Tara's Magical World

Chandra Ghosh Jain

Tara's Magical World

Copyright © Chandra Ghosh Jain 2024

ISBN: 978-93-94437-90-6

This book has been published with all reasonable efforts taken to make the material error-free after the consent of the author. No part of this book shall be used, reproduced in any manner whatsoever without written permission from the author, except in the case of brief quotations embodied in critical articles and reviews.

The Author of this book is solely responsible and liable for its content including but not limited to the views, representations, descriptions, statements, information, opinions and references ["Content"]. The Content of this book shall not constitute or be construed or deemed to reflect the opinion or expression of the Publisher or Editor. Neither the Publisher nor Editor endorse or approve the Content of this book or guarantee the reliability, accuracy or completeness of the Content published herein and do not make any representations or warranties of any kind, express or implied, including but not limited to the implied warranties of merchantability, fitness for a particular purpose. The Publisher and Editor shall not be liable whatsoever for any errors, omissions, whether such errors or omissions result from negligence, accident, or any other cause or claims for loss or damages of any kind, including without limitation, indirect or consequential loss or damage arising out of use, inability to use, or about the reliability, accuracy or sufficiency of the information contained in this book.

Publisher

Books Mantra Publications
(An imprint of Clever Fox Publishing)
www.booksmantra.com

For

Tara, Avyaan and Vir
They have created magic for me

Written by
Chandra Ghosh Jain (Dadi).
2024
Jaipur

One bright sunshiny afternoon Tara lay on the grass in her garden. She saw a very pretty large butterfly. It was red, coloured with yellow dots. Tara called out to her "Titli Rani come sit besides me".

She replied, "You come with me -I will show you the magical world."

Tara ran after her but Titli Rani had flown higher and higher in the sky. Tara shouted "Wait, wait" she was huffing and puffing.

A cloud came floating by and Tara jumped on to it. It was soft and comforting. Titli Rani came and settled down near her.

Soon Tara saw a huge big whale floating by.

The Blue Whale had a very happy smile on his face. Tara called out "Blue Whale Bhaiyaa, how come you are here?"

"Oh! I was tired of being in the water all the time. I wanted to fly in the sky."

With that he plonked himself on the cloud.

Tara said, "I will climb on your back so that I have a higher view of the earth below."

Soon she saw a Mother Bird crying out, 'Chi, chi, chi where have my little birds gone?"

Blue whale called out, "Don't worry Mamma, I will get them. They are flying after some beautiful butterfly."

Soon Tara spotted a bright pink coloured star fish with a very happy smile. Blue whale called out, "What are you doing here?"

She winked and said, "what else, having lots of fun!" The sea weeds floating beside her swayed in agreement.

"Come jump in and join Tara's Gang!" Called out Blue whale.

"In the forest nearby I had seen a Mamma Dragon with two eggs. Do you want to go there Tara? asked the Star fish.

Tara, agreed, "Yes". She was looking forward to the new fascinating adventures with her magical friends.

As Tara's cloud floated on to a tree top, she noticed the baby dragons coming out of their eggs. They were rather hungry.

"Ma, ma, ma - doodh, doodh" - they were calling out. They were scratching Mamma dragon's feet.

The dragon mother was looking puzzled. "Where will I get milk from? Whoever has heard of dragon babies drinking milk? Eat grass, insects."

"Don't worry Mamma, I have a 'Mausi' in a nearby village. She has a big black buffalo who gives lots of milk," said the star fish.

The Dragon Mamma picked up her babies and flew along with the starfish.

Gradually the sky darkened, the Sun had sunk and vanished. A bright full moon shone in the sky. Tara found herself staring at an Octopus who waved his arms, 'Hi' he said. Tara called out, 'Hi'.

He jumped on to her cloud followed by a sea-horse who had decided to become a sky-horse. And a Turtle who was old and wise. 'Hungry?' he asked. Tara nodded and almost immediately fell off to sleep.

When she awoke she found herself looking into a fairy on the lawn."

"Oh! I had been waiting for you for so long."

"I am hungry - very hungry," Tara exclaimed.

"Ah! This is my garden, my home," exclaimed Tara.

The fairy smiled, "you go in and get your food."

Tara looked scared, "No, no my Mamma will be very angry with me. So will my Papa. They will ask where I had been all night."

She looked at the fairy, "Pari didi, please you go quietly in and get me something to eat."

Tara was soon gorging on Chhole Bhature, Chocolate cake and gajar- ka-Halwa. She washed it down with a tall glass of milk.

With a satisfied smile and a milky Moustache Tara looked around.

"Oh! There is a new pot in my lawn!" But the pot was tilted. All attempts to set it straight failed.

Tara looked at the pot, there was Maa Durga Carved and painted on it.

Maa Durga called out in a serene Voice, "Tara I have magical leaves. If you eat the small ones, you will grow very big. And if you nibble on the big ones you will grow tiny."

Tara stuffed her right pocket with the small leaves. And her left pocket with The Large leaves. Then she jumped on her cloud and flew away..

Soon her gang joined her - starfish, Blue Dolphin and her old friend Titli Rani.

Tara saw a snail move past her, he said or rather whispered, "Hi! I also want to join your gang."

"Yes of course, you are most welcome!" Tara clapped her hand in joy as The Snail settled in her lap. He whispered," "I saw the two baby dragons swimming in the sea near the village".

Soon they floated near the sea. There was Mamma Dragon, weeping and crying as she saw her babies Swim further and further away.

Star fish held her hand, "Don't worry Mamma, we will get them back."

The baby dragons had grown big & large after drinking the milk. Mamma Dragon couldn't swim.

Tara chewed the tiny leaf and soon grew very large. So did the Snail.

Tara with the help of now-huge snail made two big ropes with the Leaves. She instructed the sea weeds to swim along with her.

Soon all of them, including the octopus neared the dragons, who were splashing around. Mamma dragon held one end of the rope, and with the other Tara, Blue-whale wrapped the arms and Legs of one dragon. Meanwhile, the sea weeds wrapped themselves on their eyes. When he opened his eyes to cry, Tara quickly slipped the big leaf in his mouth. Soon, he stopped thrashing around and grew his tiny normal size. Then Mamma Dragon scooped him in her arms.

Tara swam back to the other dragon who was struggling between Star-fish, octopus and the snail. Tara slipped another big leaf in his Mouth and within a moment he shrank to his normal small size. Mamma dragon just picked him by the ear and flew away.

Tara sighed and chewed on the large leaf and offered one to the Snail.

The cloud drifted towards Tara's house. The sky had darkened and as Tara nodded off to sleep she saw the star-fish wink at her as she drifted away…

Tara this was the original Star-Fish and Baby dragons and Mamma dragons I had drawn.

www.ingramcontent.com/pod-product-compliance
Lightning Source LLC
LaVergne TN
LVHW070939070526
838199LV00035B/658